ROSE'S ROYAL MIDGETS
AND OTHER LITTLE PEOPLE
OF VAUDEVILLE

DEDICATION

To all the talented Little People
throughout the ages who have performed
in theatres, carnivals, circuses, town halls.
Thank you!

ISBN 978-0-578-76252-4

FIRST EDITION

Book design by Noah Diamond

Printed in the United States of America

vaudevisuals.com

ROSE'S ROYAL MIDGETS
AND OTHER LITTLE PEOPLE
OF VAUDEVILLE

essays by
TRAV S.D.

foreword by
JAMES TAYLOR

— VAUDEVISUALS PRESS —

NEW YORK

"*I am convinced that the only people worthy of consideration in this world are the unusual ones. For the common folks are like the leaves of a tree, and live and die unnoticed.*"

— THE SCARECROW OF OZ,
from *The Marvelous Land of Oz*
by L. Frank Baum

Perfomer Gladys Farkas, who appeared with the Rose's Royal Midget troupe during her career in show business. See Chapter III.

CONTENTS

ACKNOWLEDGMENTS

I wish to express thanks to my wonderfully talented friends who helped make this book happen: Trav S.D., James Taylor, and Noah Diamond, without whom this book would not be possible.

To my beautiful wife, Deborah, for her patience in putting up with my late night / early morning work schedule.

To Benjamin Taylor of LitRiot Press, for his time in walking me through the process of publishing a book; and Thom Wall of Modern Vaudeville Press, for helpful advice. To Laurette Harris for help in editing the Preface.

To my good friend and professional clown/juggler Karen McCarty (co-founder and co-director of Healthy Humor, Inc.) and her mother Annabelle Waldman, for their invaluable contribution to this book. Their photographs, letters, and interviews have made this a very personal project.

To Grace Wagner and Nicole Westerdahl of the Special Collections Research Center at Syracuse University Library, for their assistance with the Ronald G. Becker Collection of Charles Eisenmann Photographs.

To Peter Shrake of Circus World in Baraboo, Wisconsin, for his help with photographs from that collection.

All photos are courtesy of the Vaudevisuals Archive,
except where otherwise noted.

PREFACE

S itting on my desk is a small, dark green souvenir program with crumbled corners and brittle paper. *Life History of Rose's Twenty-Five Royal Midgets* is the banner headline. Purchased at an auction with other vaudeville memorabilia, it grabbed my attention. I knew next to nothing about this company, but the cover illustration of the company members drew me in. I wanted to know more.

A few things that happened along the way helped make this book a reality. I contacted two people I knew would be interested and would know about this subject. Trav S.D., who pens the terrific blog Travalanche and wrote *No Applause – Just Throw Money: The Book That Made Vaudeville Famous*, had written about Rose's Royal Midgets, as well as many other performing companies of Little People. I requested his participation.

James Taylor, who writes and publishes the sideshow world's own *Shocked and Amazed* books, was another friend and personality I asked to contribute. He wrote the Foreword to this book.

As I was collecting vintage postcards of Rose's Royal performers to help illustrate this book, I mentioned the project to my good friend Karen McCarty. A professional clown, Karen had worked for years in the circus. Years ago, she had mentioned that her grandmother was in vaudeville. Now I discovered that her grandmother, Gizella Farkas (renamed Gladys in America), was a member of Rose's company!

When I interviewed Karen and her mother Annabelle Waldman (the daughter of Gladys Farkas), they brought this story so much closer than I had ever imagined. They supplied me with photographs and personal letters from throughout Gladys's career. And I had the privilege of photographing the custom-made shoes and gloves Gladys wore in performances.

Thus, a potpourri of beautiful and rare images illustrates this story of an extraordinary company, which was an important part of America's performing arts history.

JIM R. MOORE
Publisher

FOREWORD

BY JAMES TAYLOR

It means...

I once got hate mail from a Munchkin. I'm not using that term in any way pejoratively nor as some sort of "dog whistle" (to use the terminology of this era) any more than I'd use the terms *midget, freak,* nor *sideshow.* And I'm not going to contend that those terms shouldn't raise hackles when used outside their express realm: the old-time novelty and variety business, for types of acts, styles of performance, modes of "style" in a staged setting. Drawing that distinction, though, doesn't mean that those terms don't still create problems, even among those who work the acts, work within the business, make their money and know what those expressions mean.

In the very early 1990s, I began work on *Shocked and Amazed! On & Off the Midway,* the world's first journal devoted to circus and carnival sideshows and the world of novelty and variety show biz. It was built less as a journal and more as the peri*odd*ically published volumes of a bottomless encyclopedia of "weirdness as entertainment," as showman Fred Olen Ray once put it so pointedly. And, eventually, *Shocked and Amazed!* led to a lot of media attention, in person and on screen and in print for those of us building the project. Which led, ultimately, to the producers of the *Jerry Springer Show* to catch up with me about doing an episode on talent who worked sideshow. And while I knew full well that what they meant ultimately was freak performers – especially those from the "golden age" between the World Wars – I recommended a slew of talent to them: from "born freaks" (those born with physical differences from the "norm"); "made freaks" (most commonly, heavily tattooed people, at least in the old days); and even "working acts" (typically, magicians, swordswallowers, fire manipulators, the list is long). And, as I and most who concentrate on the "big tent" which is "sideshow," I put them onto the gamut of novelty and variety talent, from Jeanie Tomaini, billed in her day as the World's Only Living Half Girl; to Percilla Bejano, who showed as the Monkey Girl; to the son and daughter of Grady Stiles, the Lobster Boy, infamously murdered by other members of the family; and to Melvin Burkhart, perhaps the most famous working act of his era, the Original Human Blockhead, so labeled by Robert Ripley himself.

And I recommended another novelty talent to Springer's people: Karl Slover, who played in 1939's *The Wizard of Oz* and was one of the last Munchkins still alive. And because we had a mutual friend – "Diamond Jim" Parker, once a clown on the "Big One," Ringling Bros., Barnum & Bailey – and because I'd gotten both Slover's and his pal Parker's okay to contact him, I referred Springer's producers to Slover. I'd interviewed Karl for *Shocked and Amazed!* months before, and I knew his background working in "midget villages" which were featured at world's fairs as well as state fairs and wherever other spots the show owners could get them booked. *The Wizard of Oz* producers,

WIKIMEDIA COMMONS

Karl Slover in 2006

in fact, had had to scour the earth for Little People to fill out the huge number of roles available in the film, so nearly every midget village troupe was pulled into the production. And, for my part, I knew full well that Springer's show was going to be looking for – and needing – novelty and variety talent of every stamp. And they would likely confront the same problem the *Oz* producers had faced: the need to "fill out" the bill for their show with novelty and variety talent, generally. So Karl Slover and every other "golden age" novelty and variety act I was connected to and/or had interviewed all got referred to Springer's producers. And my line to the performers was that they'd all need to cut their own deals, to "take their best holt" as they say in the business, get the most they could wrangle from the producers. After all, I wasn't an agent and I wasn't a booker: I was just the guy between Springer's producers and their having to do even more work tracking folks down. And if I could get the old-time talent a new payday, all to the good.

Unknown to me, though, was how the producers would frame the show. I had given them the three essential conditions, conditions I'd insisted on before I'd even referred them to any of the performers: Springer would come to them, in Gibsonton, Florida, where they were all located; there would be no audience aside from crew; and they'd all be paid. Somewhat surprisingly, the producers agreed. And I – like somebody who'd never done media, apparently – thought it'd be pretty clear sailing for all concerned except for the day-of problems that invariably crop up in show production. And so it seemed. It was a great few days, seeing performers whose years of retirement I'd tried to help make even more memorable via *Shocked and Amazed!*, performers for whom I thought I'd help get a bit of a payday while they answered questions about a long-gone era in the business, a business I knew they'd all enjoyed and enjoyed talking about. What glitches there were during the shoot were, typically, logistical. Everybody seemed happy to take part, patient to be available when the crew ran late or had to reschedule, more than agreeable to be directed from mark to mark. Karl Slover, for his part, appeared only briefly when the episode aired, standing with Melvin Burkhart laughing, in amused astonishment, watching Burkhart do the act he'd made famous: The Human Blockhead.

And when the episode aired, it aired as *I Worked as a Sideshow Freak*. And everybody looked great: Springer did them all justice, handling the talent the way all talent would want to be and presenting them that way as well: respectfully, as fellow show business talent in a once hugely popular performance mode. And, for a week or three afterwards, the feedback to me was 101% positive from all those who appeared on screen. And then I

The Wizard of Oz (1939)

got Slover's letter. You see, as he contended in his letter, he never worked a "sideshow" nor worked as a "freak"; he worked in a *midget village*, the implication throughout his letter being that such terminology applied to him was pejorative, disrespectful. I have to admit, it wasn't just his ire over the title of the episode (a direction taken by Springer's producers, I'm sure, to grab attention) that was surprising. More surprising was Slover's approach to what was now framed as an insult, an insult for having been associated with both terms: sideshow and freak, both show terms of his era, terms I thought he understood in the context of the outdoor novelty and variety business he worked, terms that in my readings and in my interviews – within the context of the acts – should've raised no ire in Karl nor any of the talent, not at all.

Clearly, I was unaware of all the facts, certainly as they applied to Karl Slover, especially as that episode finally played out. Pretty quickly after that letter's arrival, before I walked into a mine field with Slover personally, I contacted Parker, who'd brokered my original connection with Karl. And yes, he'd heard about the blowback…which had not occurred after Slover had watched the episode; at that point, at first airing of the episode, per Diamond Jim Parker, Karl had been pretty happy: He'd gotten on-air time and a screen credit and he'd gotten a payday. Sadly, however, his friends had thought otherwise (no, they were not, apparently, fellow Little People nor show people); those friends told Slover he should be p.o.ed over his "treatment" at the hands of "whoever" was "responsible." Apparently, that boiled down to me. And I'm not trying here to alibi my way out of anything, truly; in fact, I'll say that I'm glad – yes, glad – that I got that letter, that hate mail. One of the most amazing (and – referencing that letter – treacherous) things about the novelty and variety biz is its terminology. And its application. And misapplication. Freak? Sideshow? Midget? Outside of the business, those terms mean many things to many people. Those terms mean things – many different things – to those inside the business as well, apparently. And when those worlds slam into one another? Especially when there's money and attention involved?

I responded to Slover's letter, trying as best I could to explain that his complaints needed to be directed at the producers, that directing them at me missed the point as I'd nothing to do with the production beyond referrals, but I knew it would likely fall on deaf ears. Besides, I was missing the point, too: Those words do mean things. Many things. To many people. Different people. For many different reasons. The real questions, apparently, boil down to: What do those words mean to *you?* Moreover: Why?

June 2020

THREE   BRIGHT   LIGHTS
With *Rose's 25 Midgets*

Frieda   Marie   Gladys

I.
ROSE'S ROYAL MIDGETS

BY TRAV S. D.

Rose's Royal Midgets is one of those names for a vaudeville act that old time show biz fans particularly cherish, like **Fink's Mules**, or **Swayne's Cats and Rats**. As James Taylor sagely points out in his foreword, by common consent, we no longer use the term "midget" any more in civilized discourse. The people being described really don't like it. Nowadays they prefer the term "Little People", because in point of fact they *are* people, self-aware sensitive human beings, not at all like mules, cats, or rats who don't notice when they're being laughed at. We respect that, and will use their preferred term when describing people of small stature. But we must warn you up front about one exception that must unavoidably be made. In the late 19th century and early 20th centuries, in addition to its common usage, "midget" was a term of art in the show business world, and was included as part of the professional names of many show business acts. When we reference these acts, or when such performers are mentioned in quotations, we'll need to dig up the outmoded term for the sake of clarity. Just so you know.

There were many traveling troupes of Little People back in the day.

17

Some of them include **Singer's Midgets** (most famous for supplying many of the Munchkins for *The Wizard of Oz*), **Klinkhart's Troupe of Midgets, Hermine's Midgets, Horvath's Midgets, The Rossow Midgets**, and **The Murray Midgets**. But there was something that set the Rose act apart. Before it had even been founded, the Rose name meant something.

Ike Rose (Isaac S. Rosenstamm, 1865-1935) was a show business legend decades before he launched his famous act. He was considered one of the top impresarios of his day, on a par with men like **Tony Pastor** and **Florenz Ziegfeld**. In the early years of his career, Rose had booked and represented some of the top variety acts of the late 19th and early 20th centuries, including **Harry Houdini, Chung Ling Soo** (William Robinson), **Ruth St. Denis, The Hilton Sisters**, and his greatest creation, an international star known as **Saharet**. Rose's contemporaries would be astounded to learn that posterity would remember this showman foremost not for promoting those famous acts, but instead a troupe of Little People, a kind of lark with which he occupied his twilight years.

Born in Hanover, Germany, Rose immigrated to the U.S. with his family when he was six months old, growing up in the Kleindeutschland or "Little Germany" section of New York's Lower East Side. On a passport his father's occupation is given as "German teacher."

By 1886, Ike was writing for the *Police Gazette*, a popular and colorful magazine that covered true crime, sports, and show business (with a particular interest in burlesque). In what was then a frequent career path, Rose then made the jump from journalist to p.r. man to impresario. **Ned Buntline** had gone this very same route in making a star out of **Buffalo**

Billy Cody. By 1890 Rose had become, in the words of the *New York Clipper*, the "hustling advance man" for variety man **Gus Hill** (Gustave Metz, 1858-1937). Like Rose, Metz had grown up in New York's German section. His stage name was taken from **Harry Hill's Saloon**, a notorious Manhattan resort, and he got his start in show business as a juggler, wrestler, and Indian club twirler. By Rose's time he'd begun producing vaudeville revues he called *Gus Hill's Novelties*, where he presented performers like the young comedy team of **Weber and Fields** on bills with himself. Early in the 20th century, he was to become one of the founders of the **Columbia Burlesque Wheel** and one of the most powerful men in show business. Hill and Rose would be friends and colleagues for at least three decades. Hill would in fact be instrumental in establishing Rose's Royal Midgets in the United States, though there would be much water under the bridge before that happened.

By the mid 1890s, Rose was working as ringmaster and "general man" for **The Irwin Brothers Circus**. Originally from England, the Irwin Brothers (George, Jacob, Fred, Bill and James) were a Buffalo-based

Annabelle Waldman, whose mother performed with the troupe (See "Gladys Farkas" chapter), has kindly identified the personnel in this photograph: "L. to R.: Vance Swift (James Vance Swift), Adella Novack, Susanna Bokonyi (oldest, from Hungary), Esther Howard (black singer), Florence Novak, Gussie Pick (from Germany), Nita Krebs, Alice Pick (from Germany), Jacqueline Hall (as Mae West), Freddie Ritter (on violin), Gene Palfie (musical director), Vivian (can't remember last name), Steve Casper (on sax), Tony Vandola (on drums)."

Ike Rose and company, 1920s

acrobatic and equestrian act that performed balance stunts, feats on the trapeze and horizontal bars. In their early years they had performed with the **Dan Rice, John Robinson**, and **Forepaugh** shows. The Irwin Brothers Circus was formed in 1887. The most famous of the bunch would come to be **Fred Irwin**, founder of **Irwin's Burlesquers**, with whom **W.C. Fields** performed around the turn of the century. Like Gus Hill, Fred Irwin was one of the architects of the Columbia Wheel. The other Irwin Brothers went on to splinter into other acts and shows of their own over the decades. Rose was with the circus roughly from 1894 to 1895.

Early 1896 proved to be a time of seismic shift in Rose's life. At that time he caught a burlesque revue called *Night Owls*, managed by **George W. Lederer**, who later married **Marion Davies**' sister and was the father of writer **Charles Lederer** (who co-wrote *The Front Page* with **Ben Hecht**, among other things). Ensconced at **Miner's Bowery Theatre**, the *Night Owls* company promised and delivered "a galaxy of pretty girls," one of whom was a bewitching dancer who went by the name of **Saharet**. Saharet was actually an Australian lass named **Paulina Clarissa Molony** (1878-1964), who came to the U.S. via San Francisco, performing initially under the unspectacular name of **Clarice Campbell**. Working her way west with burlesque pioneer **M.B. Leavitt**, she rapidly learned the ropes. The name "Saharet" was an apparent reference to the Sahara Desert, no doubt a reflection of **Little Egypt** and the belly dancing trend that had gripped the show business world since the 1893 Chicago World's Fair. Saharet was half Asian (her mother was ethnically Chinese), and was possessed of a type of beauty that was then considered "exotic" to the mostly Euro-American audience at the time. Her repertoire ranged from French quadrilles to risqué cooch and snake dances.

Smitten with what he saw, Rose quickly moved in, both professionally and romantically. He and Saharet were married that year and had a daughter, **Carolyn "Carrie" Madelon Rose** (1896-1950), herself to become a Broadway performer in the 1920s under the name **Madeline La Varre**. Under Rose's management, Saharet rapidly climbed the ladder of show business success to better venues and much higher salaries. In New York she played prestigious venues like **Koster and Bial's** and **Hammerstein's Olympia**. In 1897 she performed in the U.K. The following year it was on to Paris and Berlin. Her greatest success over the next 15 years was to be on the Continent, although she continued to return to the U.S. and London for engagements as well. Huge sums were made by the pair during this period.

Rose leveraged his success with Saharet into a more diversified career. Whereas peers like **Martin Beck** and **Flo Ziegfeld** were respected for bringing European stars back to the U.S., Rose became known as the foremost American impresario in Europe, famed for bringing Yankee performers to the Old World Capitals. By 1900 he was booking variety shows at the **Wintergarten Theatre** in Berlin, featuring acts like the escape artist **Houdini**, magician **Chung Ling Soo** (for whom some credit Rose with devising his stage name), the comedy team of **Lowell and Lowell, Eckard the Hoop Roller,** and a singing act called **The Four Emperors**.

After a decade together, Saharet and Rose grew apart as a couple, although Rose continued to manage Saharet's career, even as he continued to build his roster of clients. We know that he represented the great modern dancer **Ruth St. Denis** prior to 1910 because that year he sued her in a London court for unpaid commissions. In 1912 he took over

Ike Rose with some of his stars

management of **The Hilton Sisters,** a famous pair of conjoined twins who later appeared in the 1932 movie *Freaks*. He toured with The Hilton Sisters throughout Germany, the U.K. and Australia, at one point presenting them on a bill with **The Blazek Twins,** another pair of conjoined sisters, a show business first. Apparently this was too much for Saharet, who dropped Rose as both a manager and a legal spouse in 1913. But by this time, Rose had another ace up his sleeve: Little People.

The premiere presenter of diminutive humans in the modern age was of course **P.T. Barnum,** who made an international splash starting in 1842 with his celebrated displays of two-and-a-half foot tall **Charles Stratton** a.k.a. **General Tom Thumb**. Stratton helped make a pile of money for Barnum, and became one of the richest men in the country himself. His success led to a long string of similar performers at Barnum's **American Museum** over the next couple of decades. By the 1870s, when Rose was growing up, New York's Lower East Side was rife with dime museums run by aspiring Barnums such as **George Bunnell** and **E.M. Worth**. Famous Little People were part of every bill.

The next logical plane for showmen to explore was volume. If one or two Little People were a spectacle, what about entire troupes of them? Starting around 1876, an entrepreneur named **Harry Deakins** toured nationally with **Deakins Lilliputian Comic Opera Company,** which starred several Barnum alum such as **Commodore Nutt** and "Scottish Queen" **Jennie Quigley**. This in turn led to several competing Lilliputian Opera Companies over the next couple of decades, including

MIDDLEBOROUGH HISTORICAL MUSEUM

GENERAL TOM THUMB

one owned, operated by, and starring Tom Thumb's widow **Lavinia Warren** and her second husband **Count Primo Magri**. There was also the **Locke and Davis Royal Lilliputian Company**, which starred **Admiral Dot**, and may have been the inspiration for Rose's use of the word "Royal" in his own company's name.

By 1893, the World's Columbian Exposition in Chicago could boast of an entire Midget City, where numerous Little People lived and worked under the constant gaze of gawkers. A little over a decade later showman **Samuel Gumpertz** brought the idea to **Dreamland** at **Coney Island** on a semi-permanent basis as Lilliputia, or Midget City. It was one of the public's favorite attractions. Sadly, Dreamland burned to the ground in 1911. Perhaps it was not coincidental that around the same time **The Prater** in Vienna offered its own Midget City display. It's possible that some of the displaced Coney performers crossed the puddle to work there. It is not known if this display at the famous Viennese amusement park is what specifically set Rose on his own quest to start a similar company of his own, although this is definitely what inspired the **Baron Leopold von Singer** to start Singer's Midgets at around the very same time.

As Europe exploded into the conflagration of World War One, Rose returned to the States with a company of Little People he'd hired in Austria, Hungary, Poland, Germany, France, Belgium, Italy, Java, and the United States. Rose's company had a core troupe of 25 performers, including jugglers, acrobats, impressionists, musicians, singers, and sketch comedians. There was a saxophone sextette and miniature versions of popular vaudeville teams like **Gallagher and Shean,** and **Jack Norworth and Nora Bayes.** Soprano **Hansi Herman** was considered the star of the troupe, and she was also its principal dressmaker. **Prince Pani,** from faraway Java was another standout. One newspaper made the preposterous claim (probably originating with Rose) that Pani was "the only colored midget in the world". Irrespective of his advertised uniqueness, Pani's exotic appearance and Javanese dances no doubt distinguished him within the company. **The Glauer Brothers** (Paul, Adolph, Bruno and Henry) made up an entire contingent. In the 1920 they split off and formed the U.K.-based **Glauer's Royal Midgets** with a company of 20. Much later, Paul Glauer would be one of the stars of **Werner Herzog**'s 1970 film *Even Dwarfs Started Small.*

Ike Rose and the Rose's Royal Midgets company visiting the White House in 1924

After building the act in London and Paris, Rose appears to have brought it back to the U.S. circa 1916. They were booked with much fanfare on the **Klaw and Erlanger** circuit the following year. For the next decade and a half, Rose's Royal Midgets were a vaudeville staple. In 1922 they played the **Loew's Circuit,** then known as top of the line small-time vaudeville. That same year, a *Variety* item mentioned that Rose and his old pal Gus Hill were pitching an all-midget circus complete with miniature animals. The following year, the act toured Gus Hill's vaudeville circuit with an

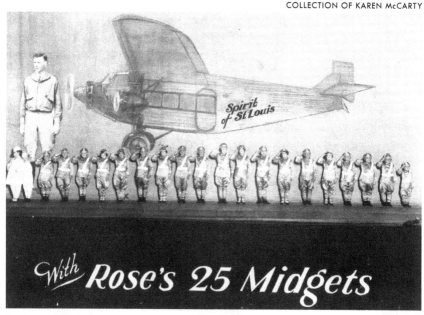

With Rose's 25 Midgets

Rose's troupe performing their tribute to Lindbergh, 1929

enhanced troupe featuring 35 members. This *Variety* announcement and the ensuing tour may be what gave rise to the common misconception that Rose's Royal Midgets dated only to 1922.

Rose's knack for publicity generating stunts got him much ink during the Roaring Twenties, as when he staged a "Midgets for Coolidge" campaign event in 1924 and a special tribute to **Charles Lindbergh** in 1929. By the end of the decade, the act was playing the **Keith-Orpheum Circuit,** the biggest of the big time.

As the years went on, the personnel in the troupe turned over. **Marie Hartline** was with Rose's Royal Midgets from 1929 through 1932. Years later she would marry **Meinhart Raabe,** the Little Person who played the Munchkin Coroner

Vance Swift
Smallest American Man
with
ROSE'S ROYAL MIDGETS

in *The Wizard of Oz*. Another favorite was **Vance Swift**, who stood 29 inches tall, was a burlesque comic, and played the xylophone. Other performers in the troupe during the '30s included **Victor Bump** and **Gladys Farkas**, and **Mary Ellen Burbach** (later to marry the Munchkin **Parnell St. Aubin**).

Vaudeville died in the early '30s. Ike Rose did not long outlive it, passing away in 1935. The management of the show then passed to Ike's second wife **Carla**, who was invariably mentioned in the press as "**Mrs. Ike Rose.**" With vaudeville gone, the troupe played venues like the 1932 Winter Olympics, the 1933 Chicago World's Fair, the 1935 California Pacific International Exposition, the 1936 Texas Centennial Exposition, and the 1939 New York World's Fair.

In 1938 Carla Rose ran a full page ad in *Billboard* announcing the new edition of the show, now called **Rose's Parisian Midget Follies,**

IKE ROSE'S ROYAL MIDGETS
AND THE ONLY MIDGET BAND IN THE WORLD
BROKE EVERY RECORD IN THE MARCUS LOEW THEATRES

First week in Lent, Newark; Christmas week, Victoria, New York; New Year's week, 86th Street, New York, and the biggest business ever done in the history of the Orpheum, Boston, Holy Week, turning them away four shows daily Holy Thursday and Good Friday.

NOW PLAYING INDEPENDENT HOUSES

On percentage and guarantees to turn away business with the most talented Midget Show ever seen in this country.

Address IKE ROSE

THIS WEEK (SEPT. 10)—COMMUNITY THEATRE, MERIDEN, CONN.
NEXT WEEK (SEPT. 17)—CENTRAL THEATRE, JERSEY CITY

Variety, September 13, 1923

which featured midget versions of **Mae West, Bill Robinson, Harriet Proctor, Morton Downey, Ethel Waters** and a company of hillbillies. The following year *Family Circle* magazine published an entire feature on the show, concentrating especially on Carla, Swift and Burbach (who was the midget Mae West in the show).

During the 1940s and '50s, carnivals, fairs, and circuses kept the troupe going. In 1941 and '42 they were booked with the **Beckmann and Gerety Shows**. In the late '40s they traveled with **Al Wagner's "Cavalcade of Amusements,"** a huge carnival show that traveled on 54 train cars. In 1948 Carla Rose and several members of the troupe were injured in a train wreck as they traveled with that show. In the 1950s, they rode with **Wallace Brothers Circus**. A 1954 item *Billboard* mentions that two members of the troupe, **Slovenia Jennie Riddle** and **Anthony Vendola,** had gotten married. In 1957 Rose's Royal Midgets performed with the **Grotto Circus**. The last mention of the show as a going concern we have uncovered is in 1959.

Two years prior to that (1957), **Billy Barty** had founded his advocacy group **The Little People of America**. This organization helped transform public attitudes about the exhibition of small statured performers. There are still hundreds of Little People in show business, but it's a different culture, with different expectations. One wonders what Ike Rose would have made of it all. My instinct is that, like all successful impresarios, he was an adapter who knew how to change with the times. Something tells me that he would have found a respectful way to hire **Peter Dinklage**.

ROSE'S
MIDGET
REVUE

Annabelle Waldman has identified the personnel in these photographs. Above: "Men are Vance Swift in front, Tony Vandola with horn, Gene Palfé on drums, Steve Gasper on sax. Women are Susanna to the left; Esther up front; Jackie as statue with Adella and Gussie on each side; Florence, Alice, and Sonia up to the men." Below: "L. to R.: Frieda Zwiebler, Joe Crabowski (married to Frieda Zwiebler), Jackie Hall, Kurt Zwiebler, Sonja Hall, Werner Zwiebler, Esther Howard."

ROSE'S MIDGET REVUE

II.
1925
SOUVENIR PROGRAM

This section reprints, in its entirety, the promotional publication Life History of Rose's Twenty-Five Royal Midgets, *a souvenir created and distributed by the Rose company in 1925.*

Although from our modern viewpoint, we can't endorse every statement contained in the following ten pages, the program is a fascinating artifact of its era, and Rose's affection and enthusiasm for his troupe is clearly communicated.

PROGRAM

OF

Rose's 25 Midgets

**THE BIGGEST COMPANY AND BEST AND MOST
TALENTED MIDGETS IN THE WORLD**

Direct from Sensational Triumphs in London, Paris and
New York

Musical Director, Bernat Singer

1—Opening Chorus .... Ensemble
2—Saxophone Sextette .... Musical Singers
3—Stars of Movieland .... Ensemble
4—Cycle of Songs .... Mlle. Hansi
5—Acrobatic Novelties .... Williams Company
6—Gallagher and Shean .... Paul and Adolph Glauer
7—The Midget Band .... Singer Company
8—Stepping Out .... Henry and Bruno Glauer
9—Rolling Globe .... Miss Ilonka
10—Impersonation of Sousa .... Theo. Williams
11—Jazz Interlude .... Prince Pani
12—Minuet (past and present)
Finale...................................Entire Company of 25 Midgets

Costumes, hats, furnished by Vanity Fair Costume Company, 353 West 48th St., New York City. Scenery drapes
furnished by Novelty Scenic Company, 226 West 47th St.,
New York City.

If these American, Italian, Polish, Hungarian, German
Midgets have pleased you, tell your friends to come and see
them... Send the children.

I. S. ROSE

Proprietor of Rose's Midgets

who gathered this wonderful, biggest, greatest and perfect formed Midget Show of Artists in Europe and brought them to the United States, where they have made the biggest success of any Midget Show and Company of Lilliputians ever seen in this country. Each and every one a great performer.

PAUL GLAUER
Born in Germany
28 Years Old

LENA BAYER
German
37 Years Old

PRINCE PANI
Born in Java
40 Years Old

ROSE'S ROYAL MIDGETS

Tales of the Tiny Folk

"Lovable little ladies and gentlemen, as well as gifted entertainers of remarkable talent."
—King Alfonso of Spain.

The life stories of the twenty-five doll-size men and women artists gathered from European and East Indian lands by I. S. Rose, most widely known American impressario on the Continent of Europe.

———

YEARS ago in Peter Pan, Maude Adams stood over the footlights and asked audiences of sophisticated New Yorkers, "Do you believe in fairies?" It is a matter of record that some of the tens of thousands who heard, laughed, for deep in every adult heart is a tender warmth for those childhood days when fairies and elfin folk were very real to us all. And so it is with midgets—perfectly normal miniature men and women, who just stopped growing as little children, so far as stature is concerned. And this love of fairies, this belief in their goodness and Cinderella-like deeds of kindness, is what explains the extraordinary delight that children take in midgets. It is because the tiny people are fairy book characters come to life in the minds of the children that boys and girls are drawn irresistibly to them.

———

CROWDS FLOCK ABOUT THEM

AND the quarter of a hundred little folk of Rose's Royal Midgets prove all this daily. Children flock about them happily whenever they appear on the street. They do not have to beg their parents to take them to see the midgets, either, for the attraction of the vest-pocket revue and vaudeville artists is universal. Everybody loves the midgets, and everybody goes to see them.

And why shouldn't they? Was there ever a more interesting and cunning little creature on earth than tiny Lucille, barely two feet high, a bright, cultured little woman, smaller than most French dolls, but an actress of real ability and a surpassingly graceful dancer. She is so tiny on the stage that women gasp with startled delight when she steps from the wings, yet she has the joys, sorrows, interests and ambitions that her years—she is eighteen—warrant. To the children she is a tiny proof that fairy tales are true, and to adults she is the cutest thing they ever saw.

DO THEY LOVE AND MARRY?

WHO were her parents? Were they midgets? Is she married? If not, does she take an interest in the good looking little men of the company, or does she, because of her fully grown-up mind and sensibilities, long for the love of a Valentino or an every-day man of affairs?

These are questions that pop into our minds as we gaze delightedly on the tiny princess and her comrades of this Lilliputian company.

Without exception the parents of all midgets are normal. The father of Lena Bayer is a professor of chemistry in the university at Bonn, Germany. He is five foot eight inches in height, and Lena's mother is five foot four inches. Lena has had an education that many girls of her age might envy, but she was taught privately. Where midgets are not well educated, it is generally the result of timidity, for they have not cared to go forward with their classes in public schools, watching their comrades grow away from them in stature month by month.

Lucille has a brother with the show—Hardi, barely 28 inches high, an acrobat and a dancer. He, too, is well educated. Neither he nor his sister have had any love affairs as yet, although it seems inconceivable that either will long escape Cupid's darts. However, sex attraction is not pronounced among midgets. They are, as a rule, somewhat backward in this respect, or rather, they are slow to respond to the call of sex. He is twenty years old.

SOME HAVE MARRIED

ALTHOUGH there are no members of Rose's Royal Midgets married at the present time a wedding is likely to occur before the close of the American tour, for Hansi Herman,

HERMAN ARNDT
German
25 Years Old

HANSI HERMAN
German
29 Years Old

KARL STARKE
German
24 Years Old

EXTRAORDINARY LILLIPUTIAN HUNGARIAN JAZZ BAND
Saxophone Septette. Xylophone Soloists—Only Midget Band in the World—With
Rose's Midgets. James Palfi, Leader

the leading prima donna and Herman Arndt have a very serious affair, and
it is conducted in exactly the same manner and with exactly the same
dignity that two young people in their twenties in any community in
America would conduct their romance. There have been many midget mar-
riages, but, so far as is known, none has resulted in offspring. However,
midget women have married adult men, and in one case, a normal child was
born to such a union.

While Elly and Lena, Anna, Hansi Elizabeth, Ilunka and other women
of the Rose company seem to regard the most attractive of grown-up men
with courteous indifference, all of the little men of the troupe are not so
unresponsive to the attractiveness of normally sized women. The little
men have an eye to adult (if one may use the word) feminine beauty.

Where many of
them are wholly
indifferent to the
allure of the tiny
ladies o f t h e
show, they a r e
keenly a l i v e to
the beauty of the
belles in the cit-
ies they play, and
many of the lat-
ter view the mid-
gets' infatuations
with high amuse-
ment and a sort
of flattered in-
terest. It is not
every girl that
c a n number a
midget a m o n g
her conquests!

ONLY ACROBATIC MIDGET TROUPE IN THE WORLD
WITH ROSE'S MIDGETS

PAUL and ADOLPH GLAUER
Greatest Imitators, of and by Personal Permission of Gallagher and Shean

The first midget marriage known to America was that of General Tom Thumb, who married a lady of his own size and age while on tour with P. T. Barnum. Newspapers heralded the event as of world importance, and the general and his bride were received by crowned heads abroad and dignitaries everywhere in America. General and Mrs. Thumb died without issue, however.

MIDGETS ARE NOT DWARFS

MIDGETS, let it be known, are perfectly normal in every respect, except in stature. They are just miniature men and women. All are mentally alert, perfectly intelligent as becomes their years. The Rose midgets range in height from 26 to 42 inches and in age from 20 to 41 years. Lucille is the youngest and the tiniest. Prince Pani, Javanese, is the oldest, and among the smallest. There is a dwarf comic with the show, but he is not a midget, not by any means. Dwarfs are misshapen—too large heads, too short and bowed legs, too long as to bodies. They are not always intelligent.

LITTLE PRINCE PANI

TEN years ago, Mr. Rose was touring the Isle of Java, Dutch East Indies, with a troupe of European midgets, some of whom are yet with him. Near Batavia, they saw a group of tiny Javanese children skylarking with a caraboo, a water buffalo and a beast of burden in the Malaysian countries. Among them was one little fellow, who wore the scarlet breech clout of native nobility, and Mr. Rose became interested. He approached and saw that the native child was really a midget, thirty years of age, and forced to play with little children because of his stature. The little princeling was a distant relative of a datto, hence the distinguishing loin cloth. Mr. Rose feasted the tiny fellow's family and was feasted by them. Negotiations for Prince Pani's parental permission to travel with Mr. Rose were hurried by the sight of 500 gold gulden, and, after the Dutch government officials and the datto had approved of the contracts Pani accompanied Mr. Rose to Europe. The little Javanese has been a member of the impressario's household ever since, for Prince Pani is the most lovable midget in all the world. He counts his friends

LUCY and HARDY
Polish
Smallest man and woman in the world.
Brother and sister.
18 and 19 Years Old

Henry Glauer, 40 yrs. old

Adolph Glauer, 36 yrs old

Joe Smith, 34 yrs. old
Hungarian

by the hundreds in every land in the civilized world. Say "Prince Pani" in Petrograd or in Hongkong, it is all the same. Someone will smile fondly and exclaim: "The little Javanese midget! I know him well. Where and how is he?" Although Pani comes from a Javanese family of consequence, he never wore shoes and clothes until he went away with Mr. Rose. Now he is a Beau Brummel, a bon vivant and a traveled man of the world, and every month his mother and father and all his brothers and sisters rejoice in the arrival of the registered letter that brings them Pani's story of his doings, as dictated to Mr. Rose, and a remittance of golden gulden. Now, Pani's family, once the very poor relations of the powerful Datto Burj Aljoh Mingholi, the All Serene, present the latter with their cast-off clothing. That is how the datto manages to wear tan shoes, white duck suits and carry a cane. Prince Pani is really the head of the royal house, but he doesn't know it. The datto would be the last one to deny it, so long as the stream of guldens flows Javaward, and he swells around Batavia in European clothing, even if second-hand.

A MIDGET PRIMA DONNA

HANSI HERMAN is perhaps the most attractive, the most talented and the most fashionable of the Rose midget women. She is the modiste and the Lady Duff-Gordon of the Tinyland troupe. She designs the women's gowns, following the modes of the moment in whatever country the show is in. She, like nearly all the little people, speaks three languages, is well read, and is smart as any social butterfly in New York, London, Vienna or Paris. She has beautiful brunette hair, bobbed, and she has the savior faire of Lady Diana Manners. Hansi is a prima donna of note, and she has appeared in European revues and vaudeville for several years. She is twenty-nine years of age, and is 31 inches tall.

THREE MIDGET BROTHERS

HENRY, BRUNO and PAUL GLAUER are brothers, born in Germany some thirty years ago of normally sized parents. Their father and mother are still alive on a farm in Northern Prussia. The brothers range in height from 29 to 32 inches, and all are well off financially. Just a few weeks ago Henry bought three apartment houses in Berlin, paying only $350 in American gold for a tenement building of ten two-room suites. All of the brothers are mentally keen, and are the equals of any grown-ups they encounter in a business way. All three keep in close touch with political, industrial and social conditions in Germany. They head the Rose group of musical comedy stars—singers, dancers, impersonators and light comedians. They have been performers in Europe since they were boys in ther 'teens.

HOW MIDGETS TRAVEL AND LIVE

THE ROSE Royal Midgets travel from city to city in two private cars—a sleeper and a combination baggage and observation car. In cities, where they play engagements, they do not stop at hotels, but secure apartments, where their own chefs prepare their meals. They eat a little less than half of what satisfies the average grown person. For breakfast an egg, a bit of toast and coffee; for luncheon a little chicken, a vegetable and tea, and for dinner a meat, a salad, highly seasoned, a sweet and tea suffice for the daily menu. Although the midgets could sleep comfortably six together, they will only retire two to even the largest of double beds. They are dignified little artists, and as such they live their daily lives.

WHAT CAUSES THEIR TININESS

THERE is a medical explanation for midgets' lack of growth. It is that the pituitary gland, located behind the ear, does not function. In childhood, or in babyhood, this gland atrophies, and the child fails to attain stature. Conversely, where the gland functions overtime, the child becomes a giant. It is a scientific fact that the inertia of the pituitary gland has one fortunate resultant—the midget is invested with the attribute of cheerfulness, of contentedness. All midgets are happy, and they do not regret their lack of stature. Visit with Rose's Royal Midgets backstage or in their apartments, and you chat with amiable, cheerful little people, the souls of courtesy and good breeding. They are extremely hospitable, remarkably cordial hosts and hostesses. Although their expert showmanship and stage artistry have been gained through hard work, their teachers have always found them cheerfully willing, eager to learn, so that they might make sure of a life work and a comfortable old age, free from financial worry. They are a

Bruno Glauer, 35 yrs. old
German

Karl Stephan, 25 yrs. old
German

Ilonka Blazek, 37 yrs. old
Hungarian

ELLY POPEZYK
Polish
30 Years Old

very generous, grateful little people and are never so happy as when making Mr. I. S. Rose—"our dear impressario," they call him—presents. The women are constantly doing bits of fancy work to present to Mrs. Rose, and the men buy novelties wherever they go to give Mr. Rose with dignified little speeches of presentation. And, of course, every national holiday of the midgets—they come from Hungary, Austria, Germany, Belgium, Java and France—is celebrated with a dinner backstage to the entire company of twenty-five by Mr. Rose, who looks after them as though they were the children their inches would seem to indicate.

NO MIDGET LAND ANYWHERE

SOME people imagine that there is a spot in Europe where midgets are common, where they are reared. This is not the case. The little people come from cities and towns scattered far and wide over their respective native lands. There are agents in Europe who organize them into troupes, but the contracts entered into by the agents, the parents and the midgets are supervised by the governments, so that all are protected, especially the midgets, who always remain minors under the law in all European countries. There are midgets in America, of course, but hardly any of them are artists, for those before the public are almost all in circus sideshows for exhibition purposes only. In Europe, midgets are carefully trained in the stage art, and the Rose Royal Midgets appear before the public as actors and actresses of standing and ability gained through experience in pleasing the public in almost all the countries of the globe.

To know midgets well is to love them, for they are tiny apostles of the gospel of good will. They are not temperamental. They meet all the world with a smile, and it is a perverted adult, indeed, who would trick such a lovable band of tiny ladies and gentlemen, "living dolls," who believe all the world as good as you and I would have it to smooth the paths of innocent little children.

THEODORE and HENRY
BORS
Germans, 80 and 31 Yrs. Old

40

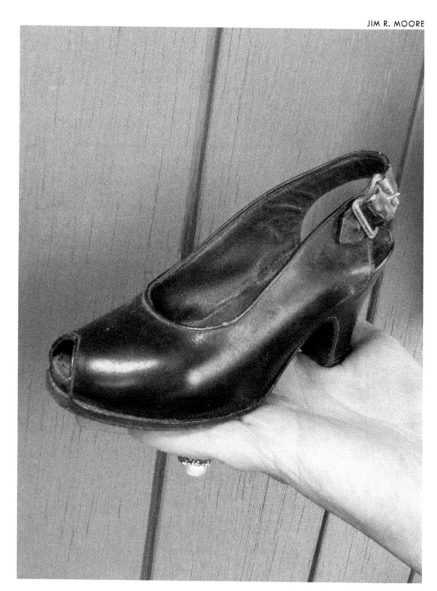

Above and opposite: Gladys Farkas's custom-made shoe and glove, shared by Annabelle and Karen and photographed by Jim R. Moore, 2020

All photographs in this chapter are courtesy of
Karen McCarty, except where otherwise noted.

III.
GLADYS FARKAS

F*ollowing are excerpts from interviews with Annabelle Waldman and Karen McCarty, the daughter and granddaughter of Gladys Farkas, conducted by Jim R. Moore in the summer of 2020.*

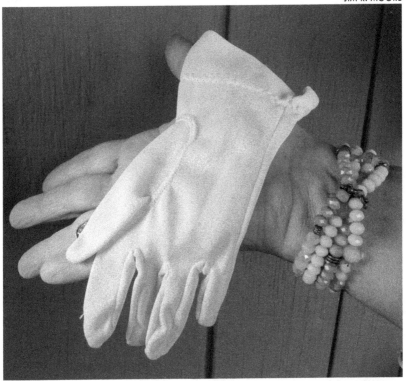

K A R E N :

Gladys Farkas came over to the USA from Hungary. She was fortunate to have been given dance and singing lessons, paid for by her mother and father. They wanted her to have special skills. They saw her talent at a young age. My grandmother was three feet and eleven inches tall. I was taller than her by the time I was five years old. Her shoes, dresses, hats...all fit me when I was four years old. This was the best "dress up trunk" from every girl's dream!

KAREN:

Mr. Rose was her first professional job. He came to her parents because he was looking for people to fill his troupe. He had contacts that knew the Hungarian arts community and knew of her. He was planning to take the company to the States, and asked her parents if she could come. He offered her $10 a week, and she said that having more skills than most of the other performers warranted she be paid more. She deserved $15. She dug her heels in and got what she wanted. She loved to tell me that story. She was so proud.

Ike Rose and his troupe, posing with the Goodyear Blimp

Gladys was the kind of person who was so small that it was startling, and she was perfectly proportioned. In other words, she was not a dwarf. She was a pituitary midget, which means that she's perfectly proportioned. She would walk into a restaurant and quiet the place in thirty seconds… she would go in and sit down, and then nod to everyone to start talking again, because they would all go quiet when she entered the room.

After she left Mr. Rose's group, she was the "Little Nightingale." Because she was the front act for the Four Nightingales (the Marx Brothers), she would go on first and sing and dance as the opening...She told me she had dated one of the Marx Brothers, but never told me which one. I always hoped it was Harpo, for my own bias!

Gladys Farkas with her husband, Victor Bump, in Peoria

Gladys at the Midget Barber Shop, part of the Midget Village exhibition at the Chicago World's Fair, 1934

C O N T R A C T

THIS AGREEMENT, made this *12th* day of *June*, 1931, between IKE ROSE, of 461 Audubon Avenue, New York City, hereinafter
designated as the "Manager" and *Miss Gladys Farkas*
hereinafter designated as Midget Artist.

W I T N E S S E T H:

WHEREAS, the parties hereto enter into an agreement this
Twelve day of *June 1931* for a period of three years, commencing
on or about September first, 1931, as a member of his Midget Company.

IKE ROSE agrees to keep *Miss Farkas* working for at least
thirty (30) weeks each year, and to pay her a weekly salary of
Fifty Dollars *For Seasons 1931 & 1932 - 1932 & 1933* a week, allow her Eight Dollars ($8.00)
each week that she is working for her food. Also to pay her hotel
bill, railroad fares, baggage, from the city of New York and return at the close of the season. *and Pay Her Season of 1933/1934*
Sixty Dollars Per Week The Manager hereby engages *Miss Gladys Farkas*
to render *Her* services exclusively to the Manager, Ike Rose, in
circuses, theatres, motion pictures and other places of amusement of every kind wherever designated by him, in any city, Mexico,
Canada, Australia.

The Midget Artist hereby accepts such employment and
agrees to render exclusively to the Manager such services as may
be required by him during the term of this agreement, upon the
terms and conditions herein set forth and agrees to appear whenever

Above and opposite: One of Gladys Farkas's contracts with Ike Rose, 1931. According to Annabelle, this was Gladys's second contract with Rose, signed after she returned from a trip to Hungary.

The Midget Artist hereby accepts such employment and agrees to render exclusively to the Manager such services as may be required by him during the term of this agreement, upon the terms and conditions herein set forth and agrees to appear whenever and wherever and in as many performances during each week as the Manager may require of him, including Sunday performances where permitted by law.

The parties hereto hereby agree that the services of the Midget Artist to be rendered and performed pursuant to this agreement are of a unique, extraordinary and special character and irreplaceable, and for said reason and in consideration of the terms of this agreement, and because of his unique and extraordinary ability, the Midget Artist agrees that for any violation or attempted violation of the provisions of this article, the Manager may apply for and secure an injunction to restrain the violation or threatened violation of the provisions of this article, to which injunction the Manager shall be entitled as a matter of right and without prejudice to or waiver of any other remedies or right that he may have either at law or in equity under this agreement.

IN WITNESS WHEREOF the parties hereto set their hands and seals the day and year first above written.

IN THE PRESENCE OF:

Elizabeth Happ

Ike Rose

Gladys Farkas

A N N A B E L L E :

Rose Kiraly (Gladys/Gizella's mother) arrived on the shores of America with her two darling daughters, only five and perhaps three. They came to Wisconsin to surprise the father of the girls. He worked at Cudahay, a meat processing plant. It turned out John Farkas was not happy that Rose and the girls arrived, and they went east again to Akron, Ohio, where she had a brother, and a sizable Hungarian community. Akron was known for rubber and Rose found work in a factory. Diptheria was a scare at that time. The younger Orna succumbed to it, but Gizella survived.

Gladys Farkas poses on the hood of a car

A physician who cared for Gizella asked if she could come to his house and join his daughter for dance classes. They danced their way into their teenage years, and one day went downtown to see vaudeville — a troupe of Little People. The girls stayed for two performances, and with Gizella's urging, made their way to the stage door. A little man, still wearing a tuxedo, greeted them and shouted down the stairs, "Mr. Rose, someone here to see you!" And that was the beginning of her career.

Rose's Royal Midgets group photo; Gladys is in the second row, center

Mr. Rose wanted to hire the little lady who said, "I can do anything your Little People can do." However, money wasn't mentioned. A correspondence grew and grew till he said "Write down what you want, I'll sign."

Gladys with some show business colleagues

300 West 42 St.
New York City
October 26, 1938

MissGladys Farkas
Congress Lake Road
R.F.D. #1
Suffield, Ohio

Dear Miss Farkas:

I am offering an engagement in Hollywood
in the production "Wizard of Oz"- one week
for trying on costumes, etc. at $25 and
3 or more consecutive weeks at $50 per
week- hotel and board, free transportation
both ways.

In case you have heard of this offer, don't
be misled by any other party; I am the only
~~xkxxxxxx~~ authorized agent for MGM to close
deals with midgets for this production.

If you are interested please answer immediately by air mail and return the enclosed
measurement sheet completelyfilled out, and
a snapshot of yourself. THIS IS VERY IMPORTANT.

Please advise me immediately, as time is
pressing.

                    Very truly your

                    Leo Singer

ls:hb

Letter to Gladys from Leo Singer, concerning MGM's film *The Wizard of Oz*. She declined to appear in the film, perhaps at the urging of her husband, Victor Bump.

HOW THE WORLD LOOKS TO A MIDGET

Gladys Farkas, Barely More Than a Yard Tall, Says Big Dogs, Ditches in the Street and Men Who Think She's a Child Are Her Pet Peeves—She Is 23, but Wears Clothing of An 8-Year-Old Child.

By Magner White

A small, petite little thing, only 42 inches tall, she smiled up at me with her intelligent grey eyes, and said, in a small voice, "Come right in!" The swagger of her dainty little form as she led the way to her dressing room at the Orpheum was something to smile about—so confident, so self-sufficient, and so essentially feminine. You've seen little girls "switch" themselves like that.

Shaking hands with Miss Gladys Farkas was like shaking hands with a baby.

"You are so tiny, I feel like picking you up to see how heavy you are," I said.

"Well," she replied, looking up and arching her eyebrows reflectively, "you would be surprised how many fresh guys try to do just that!

* * *

"That is one of the disadvantages of being a midget—everyone takes you for a child. They think because you are small, you have the mind of a child." "Why—" she stamped one of her little feet—and it sounded like the proverbial pin dripping, "—why, I'm a grown person! I am 23 years old, and have a mature mind. My feelings are just exactly the same of those of any other 23-year-old girl.

"It makes me mad when some big bozo, with a vest big enough to make me two winter coats, says, 'Hello, sweetheart'—and then starts cooing to me like I was a baby! Honestly, some men try to talk baby talk to me!" She laughed, a tinkle of a laugh.

* * *

I asked her to tell me just how the world looks to her—to a person only little more than a yard tall.

"I am used to it—but, even so, some things are fearful."

"What for instance?"

"Parades! Big dogs! Ditches in the street! When a crowd collects at a

The yard-stick gives you some idea of how tall Gladys Farkas is. Gladys, whose home is in Akron, O., is here with a theatrical company of "Lilliputians."

(Continued on Next Page, Col. 2)

This interview with Gladys appeared in the *San Diego Sun* in 1930.

HER WORLD 'AT LARGE'

From Page One

parade, I can't see a thing but hip pockets—and I do love parades.

"And an ordinary, full-grown police dog looks about as big to me as a lion does to you. I am scared of big dogs, but I like little ones—those little tiny dogs that come from Mexico. Oh, yes—I like dogs that like children, because they take me for a child.

"A ditch in the street, if its very wide, is a problem for me. To get across, I either get a nice big policeman to lift me, or I get a board and lay it across and use it for a bridge —but I prefer the policeman.

* * *

"If people could see themselves as we midgets see them, they'd diet more and take more exercise—especially men around 40 to 45. Our line of vision is about the next to the last button on the vest, and——"

She laughed mischievously, looking at Ike Ross, veteran theatrical man, and manager of the company of "Lilliputians" with whom she travels as a star. Rose has a "bay window."

"And, why don't more people shine their shoes! When we walk down a street, we can tell whether the people—the business men—in a town are tidy or not by the shoes we see.

"And, dirty streets! If all people were midgets, streets would be cleaner! Normal-height people don't notice streets so much, but we do.

* * *

"The advantages of being small are just as numerous as the disadvantages. Because we are small, and, therefore—in the eyes of 'dreat big strong peoples'—weak and helpless, people are kind to us. We get every consideration, everywhere we go.

"But, between you and me"— Gladys' eyes glowed with the intensity of the confidence she was expressing—"it gets a little tiresome to be stared at ALL the time, always to have people looking and looking and looking at you. Some of the company get quite nervous about it.

"When I was a little girl"—Gladys had wit enough to wink at that remark, as she gestured with a doll-like hand to show how little she was when she WAS little—"when I was in school, I thought out for myself what it was going to mean to be always a small person. So I don't think about it any more, and if people want to look—why, let 'em look! I see some funny humans, too.

* * *

"As soon as I'm introduced, people start asking questions. How old am I? I am 23. Are my parents small? No. Where's my home? Akron, Ohio, where I went to schol and graduated, and where my father works in the Goodrich factory. Have I any brothers and sisters? No; I'm the only child. Does 'smallness' run in our family? No; I'm the only midget. Do I mind being a dwarf? I am NOT a dwarf. I am a midget. I——"

"Pardon me—what is the difference?"

"A dwarf is a person whose normal development was arrested by some physical condition. A midget is a person who is perfectly proportioned in every way—a person just naturally small. A dwarf, with the physical condition removed, might have grown to normal size. A midget—there's no 'cure' for midgets; they're just naturally small people."

"What do you do about clothing?"

"My shoes—children's size eight—I have made to order. I like the high heels. I make my dresses—and that's where I have an advantage. I can buy the most expensive materials, and have a beautiful dress at small cost. My gloves are also made to order.

"My—ah—lingerie and pajamas; I just buy children's sizes—the 8-year-old size.

"Well, I've got to get into my make-up. I do a Russian dance, you know, and I sing and—I like this life. I'm as crazy about it as a little child!

"So long—BIG boy!"

Gladys appears third from the left in this photo of dancing Little People

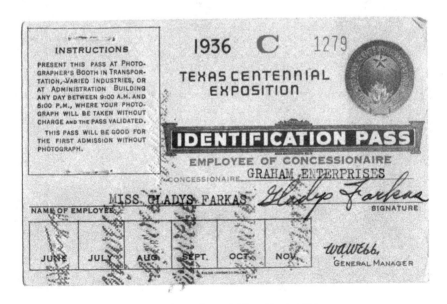

Gladys's "Identification Pass" from the Texas Centennial Exposition in 1936

Gladys models a gown created for one of Ike Rose's shows

Gizella "Gladys" Farkas

(1907 – 1991)

THOM WALL / MODERN VAUDEVILLE PRESS

Wedding portrait of Charles Stratton (Tom Thumb) and Lavinia Warren, 1863. The original caption reads: "Mr. & Mrs. 'General Tom Thumb' in their wedding costume. Entered according to an Act of Congress in the year 1863, by E. & H.T. Anthony, in the Clerk's office of the District Court of the U.S. for the So. District of New York"

IV.
OTHER LITTLE PEOPLE
OF VAUDEVILLE

BY TRAV S. D.

Some material in this chapter originally appeared on Travalanche (travsd.wordpress.com)

MR. & MRS. TOM THUMB

Charles Stratton, a.k.a **General Tom Thumb** (1838-1883) was **P.T. Barnum**'s first major success as a showman. His 1842 exhibition of the two-and-a-half foot tall Stratton resulted in North American and European tours, audiences with **Queen Victoria** and a fortune for both Barnum and Stratton. The packaging was ingenious: the clever name drawn from fairy tales, the ruse that the four year old boy was actually 11, the costuming of him as Napoleon, the funny repartee he was given to speak, the antics he was drilled to enact. The formula was repeated many times with **Admiral Dot, Commodore Nutt, Major Atom, General Mite** and others. In 1863, there was another huge burst of publicity when Stratton married fellow Little Person **Lavinia Warren** (Mercy Lavinia Warren Bump, 1841-1919) in a lavish ceremony at New York's prestigious Grace Episcopal Church. The couple arrived in a tiny custom-built wagon drawn by a small pony. Later, on their wedding tour, they met with **President Lincoln**. Stratton retired from performing in 1878; he died of a stroke 5 years later. Warren was to marry Little Person **Count Primo Magri**, and the pair toured with their own Lilliputian Opera Company.

Top: Major Dot and Countess Gallucci; bottom: Commodore Nutt and Miss Minnie Warren

The wedding of Charles Stratton (Tom Thumb) and Lavinia Warren, Grace Church, New York City, 1863

At the suggestion of P.T. Barnum, Tom Thumb and Lavinia Warren would sometimes "borrow" a baby for photographs while on tour.

THE DOLL FAMILY

The Doll Family started with a pair of siblings: **Gracie** (Freida Schneider, 1888-1970), and **Harry** (1902-1985) who began performing in German sideshows early in the twentieth century. The pair was originally billed as "Hansel and Gretel". In 1914 American impresario **Bert W. Earles** brought them to the U.S. to be in the 101 Ranch Wild West Show. Siblings **Daisy** (1907-1980) and **Tiny** (1914-2004) joined them in the act about a decade later, and for a time they all took Earles' last name for their own (they changed it to "Doll" when Earles passed away).For three decades the Doll Family appeared with the Ringling Brothers, Barnum & Bailey sideshow. From 1956 to 1958, they appeared with the Christiani Circus; then they retired. All four of the siblings appeared in the movie *The Wizard of Oz* (1939). Harry was in **Tod Browning**'s *The Unholy Three* (1925). Daisy co-starred with Harry in Browning's *Freaks* (1932) and was also in *The Greatest Show on Earth* (1952).

Sincerely, The Doll Family
Tiny — Harry — Daisy — Grace

DAISY, GRACE, TINY, HARRY

THE THREE DEL RIOS

Paul, Inez and **Trinidad Rodriguez** were a trio of miniature siblings from Spain (they also had twelve normal sized brothers and sisters). Paul, the smallest, was 19" in adulthood. Carmen, the tallest, was 33". They changed their names to the more euphonious Paul, Delores and Carmen Del Rio and began touring as an act, first in Spain, then in Mexico, and then, starting in 1935, the United States. They played the California Pacific International Exposition (1935), the Great Lakes Exposition (1936), Hamid's Million Dollar Pier in Atlantic City (1938), several places in Canada (1938-39), and the New York World's Fair (1939). They were also among the Little People hired to perform in *The Wizard of Oz* (1939). A fourth Del Rio, **Dorothy**, joined in 1944 (she may have been Paul's wife). The sisters each married musicians who were also Little People.

Princess Puppchen

Bud and Betty Bowman

KLINKHART'S MIDGETS

This troupe of Little People was managed by German born **Oscar Klinkhart** (ca.1897-1975). They were with the Al G. Barnes show between 1926 and 1931. According to some sources, they were later with Hagenbeck-Wallace Circus and got stranded near Riverside, California ca. 1936, where they founded one of the many legendary "Midgetville" communities. Later Klinkhart retired to Logsden, Oregon.

EDMOND ANSLEY

William Edmond Ansley (1891-1972) played the part of Buster Brown in personal appearance tours for Buster Brown Shoes over a period of 28 years beginning in 1910. Based on the popular comic strip character, the costume involved a long blonde wig and a Little Lord Fauntleroy suit which he wore, complete with knickers and broad brimmed hat, until he was 47 years of age. He is said to have logged 50,000 miles on the job.

EDMOND ANSLEY
WITH CHASE-LISTER CO.
SMALLEST MAN IN THE WORLD
AGE 24, WEIGHT 38 POUNDS, HEIGHT 40 INCHES

COUNT NICOL

Philippe Nicol (1881-1940) was a native of Montreal who worked for the sideshow of the Ringling Brothers and Barnum & Bailey Circus between the ages of 12 and 15. In 1906 he met fellow Little Person **Rose Dufesne**, whom he married seven years later. Having saved up large sums of money from performing, they now billed themselves as "The Count and Countess Nicol, the King and Queen of All Midgets," and opened an attraction in Montreal called The Midget Palace. Everything in the house was on a miniature scale; it was one of Montreal's top tourist attractions and it made Nicol a fortune. Apparently, the wealth didn't make its way to his son **Philippe Nicol, Jr.** (1926-1992), also a Little Person. Junior made the newspapers just once – for robbing a tobacco store in 1951. The Midget Palace was later purchased by a former employee, who kept it going until 1990.

(See Chapter V)

Le Comte NICOL, jr.

Papa veut faire de moi non pas un homme grand mais un grand homme.

Count NICOL, jr.

Papa wants me to become not a tall man but a great man.

Danny Kaye performing with Hermine's Midgets in the 1955 film *The Court Jester*

Jack and Bill

Lady Little

MR. & MRS. STANLEY JOBER

Major Stanley Jober (1883-1958) was a diminutive immigrant from Warsaw, Poland. Estimates on his height vary wildly, from 36 to 46 inches tall. His wife was 30-inch tall **Nellie Frances Way** (1884-1941), billed as "Princess Nellie", and known to be an accomplished violin player and seamstress. The pair played the Otis Smith Circus and the Mighty Doris-Col. Francis Ferrari Show. They toured the country for years in a specially customized truck, eventually retiring to Waterford, Connecticut when the Depression hit in the 1930s. They lived in a specially built miniature house, the foundation of which measured 10 x 30 feet.

LITTLE PRINCESS SONIA
LEONARD, SEMON & SONIA
MR. & MRS. FRANKS

Leonard and Sonia Franks performed with John Lester's Midgets at the Tower in Blackpool. Their 1929 marriage attracted a lot of publicity. Later they were billed as the Mayor and Mayoress of Midget Town and appeared at Battersea Festival Gardens. At one point they were joined in the act by a third partner, one **"Semon."** Sonia (sometimes spelled Sonja) was said to have been skilled as a ballerina, and to have performed with Rose's Royal Midgets.

Princess Sonia

The Great Versatile Midgets
Leonard, Semon & Sonia
and Two Yards of Human Assistance.
In Conjuring, Bending, Dancing,
Whistling, Song and Patter

The Famous Midget Bridal Couple—Mr. and Mrs. Franks.
JOHN LESTER'S MIDGETS, TOWER, BLACKPOOL.

An assortment of historical images featuring Little People in show business, including Zeynard's Liliput-Specialty Troupe, Midget Joe, George and Ida Chesworth, Mr. and Mrs. Caspar Weis, Baron Nowak, and Midgets Colibris.

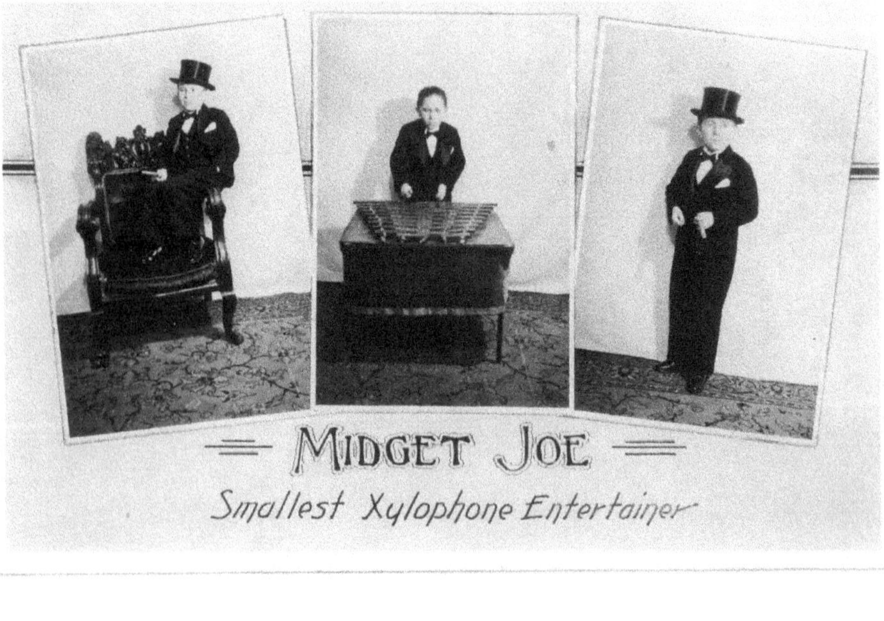

TROUPE OF MIDGETS COLIBRIS.

THE SMALLEST AND NICEST LOOKING INTELLIGENT ARTISTES
Singers, Dancers, Gymnasts Equilibrists, Illusionists
Under the direction of Professor ANTONIO.

HAROLD PYOTT

Harold Pyott (1887-1937) hailed from Greater Manchester, England. Orphaned at age 12, he fell into the keeping of an Edinburgh cousin who became his manager. Pyott played sideshows, circuses, pantomimes, music halls, and fairs for 35 years. Standing just 23 inches tall and weighing all of 24 pounds, Pyott was so small he was often the subject of publicity stunts where he was placed in someone's pocket, held in the palm of their hand, or taken for a ride atop their hat. During his career he performed throughout the UK, the Continent, and as far away as South Africa.

MR. & MRS. JEAN BREGANT

Jean Bregant (1869-1944) was originally from Cilli, Austria. In Europe he performed under the name Prince Colibri. While touring the American circuits he met his wife, **Inez Lewis** (1887-1965), also a Little Person, and they paired up for a vaudeville act and a marriage circa 1905. Bregant did the comedy chores; Inez could sing and dance. Billed as the "Candy Kids" they toured the country advertising and selling John G. Woodward candy products late in their career. They retired to Inez's home town of Council Bluffs and had a miniature house built, which still stands.

FRED ROPER
with GENERAL ROLLASON

Fred Roper was a British impresario who was a bit on the tall side, which made it look all the more impressive when he stood next to his troupe of Little People. Among Roper's accomplishments was supplying 40 Little People for Morris Gest's "Miracle Town" attraction for the 1939 New York World's Fair, making it difficult for MGM to round up the necessary number to portray Munchkins in *The Wizard of Oz* that year. Back in the '20s Roper had produced smart London revues like *The Rogues* and *The Picadilly Follies*, the latter starring his wife, mandolin player **Lillie Selden**. They also toured the British and South African music hall circuits. The troupe he billed as Fred Roper's Wonder Midgets was thirty performers strong. **"General" Edith Rollason** was 18 years old and under three feet tall at the time this postcard was made.

FRED ROPER'S WONDERFUL MIDGETS
FRED ROPER WITH GENERAL ROLLASON. 2 ft. 10 in. high. 18 years old.

EMIL RITTER'S MIDGETS

EMIL RITTER'S MIDGETS

Berlin impresario **Emil Ritter** brought his troupe of seven Little People to the U.S. in 1922, including six German nationals and one Scotsman. The idea was a vaudeville tour but apparently he forgot to get the bookings first because when they reached Ellis Island, the authorities wouldn't let him in the country, as was widely reported at the time. But they clearly made it through eventually, as the many postcard souvenirs attest.

Spread, clockwise from top left: Morris Gest's Midget Town at the New York World's Fair (1939), *Les Plus Petits Liliputiens* (The Smallest Little People), J. Jones' Midgets, and *Die Zwergenstadt mit irhen Bewohnern* (The Little People City with its Inhabitants).

Die Zwergenstadt mit ihren Bewohnern.

Souvenir
du ROYAUME DE LILLIPUT
Paris

Les plus petits LILLIPUTIENS

Master Herbert Barnett
Age 19 years

Capt. Jack Barnett
Age 39 years

HERBERT & JACK BARNETT

The Barnett Brothers, Captain Jack (1891-1935) and **Herbert** (1898-1933), hailed from Roxboro, North Carolina. Both were Little People. Jack began performing with Ringling Brothers and Barnum & Bailey when he was 16 years of age, under the name of Dainty Dewey.

Ann Margaret Robinson
World's Smallest Lady
Clyde Beatty – Cole Bros. Circus

ANN MARGARET ROBINSON

Billed as Princess Ann and The World's Smallest Lady, **Ann Margaret Robinson** is known to have performed with Clyde Beatty-Cole Brothers Circus. Standing 28 inches tall, she is said to have been with the show as late as 1973.

GLASSNER'S MIDGETS

Organized by **Rudolf Glassner,** the German act was originally billed as Glassner's Liliputaner Truppe and also known as Glassner's Musical Midgets.

HENRY KRAMER'S HOLLYWOOD MIDGETS

In the 1930s and 40s **Henry Kramer** and his wife **Dolly** put on a number of similarly named acts, the Hollywood Midgets, Midgets on Parade, The Midget Starlets, often hiring them out to movies. Members included the famous **Jerry Maren, Margaret Pellegrini** and others.

ALBERT KRAMER & SEPPETONI

Dutch giant **Albert Johan Kramer** (1897-1965), was 7 feet 9½ inches (237.5 cm) tall, while his partner and brother-in-law **Seppetoni** (Josef Fässler) was 2'10" (87 cm) tall. Ike Rose managed them both for a time in the 1920s.

ANITA, WORLD'S SMALLEST WOMAN

The British performer **Anita** was also billed as The Living Doll. She played the Hull Fair in the 1950s and in 1955 was photographed with the Lord Provost of Glasgow.

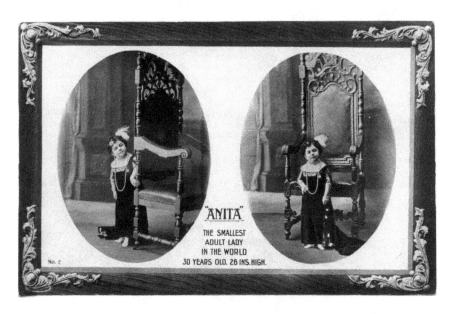

Felix Adanos and Mitzi, 1930s

CIRCUS WORLD MUSEUM, BARABOO, WISCONSIN

Members of the troupe Les Marchal Midgets, from the Johnny J. Jones Exposition, 1925

Original caption, 1924: "Charlie Becker, midget trainer with Singer's Midgets, walked the smallest elephant of his troupe to Merchant's Bank, and made a deposit for Keith's Theatre. The elephant delivered the money satchel directly to the receiving teller." Photograph by Harris & Ewing.

Coney Island, 1982

DON ROBBINS, Smallest man in the world. Forty inches high, forty-two years old

Copyrighted by Orrin J. Dickey. Publisher, Belfast, Me.

Don Robbins, circa 1900

Midget Village, Chicago World's Fair 1934: A replica of the ancient city of Dinkelsphul, Bavaria, complete with an organized city government under the supervision of Major Doyle as Mayor.

V.
1940
PHILIPPE NICOL
SOUVENIR BOOKLET

This section reprints, in its entirety, the promotional publication Biographical Sketches of Count and Countess Philippe Nicol, *a souvenir created and distributed by the New Famous Midgets Palace in 1940.*

BIOGRAPHICAL SKETCHES

CF

Count and Countess

Philippe Nicol

The King and Queen of all Midgets

THE NEW FAMOUS MIDGETS PALACE

961 RACHEL ST. EAST

VISITING HOURS : 10 A.M. to 10 P.M.

PRICE OF BOOK   :-:   :-:   :-:   25 cents

BIOGRAPHICAL SKETCHES

of

Count and Countess

PHILIPPE NICOL

King and Queen of all Midgets

and their charming baby

PHILIPPE, Junior

The only child born of Midgets.

COUNT Philippe Nicol was born at St. Henri de Lévis, P. Q., on September 27th, 1881, he is the seventh son of Alexander Nicol, who himself was also a seventh son. As all seventh sons, he is gifted with a good sense of humor, pleasantness and is a very keen business man.

The Count has six brothers and six sisters varying in height from five feet and a half to six feet. His father measures six feet three inches tall, and his mother was five feet nine inches.

From his earliest childhood, the count was remarkably small, which did not hinder

LE NOUVEAU PALAIS | THE NEW MIDGETS'
DES NAINS | PALACE

him, when he reached the age of six from attending school for three months a year.

At twelve years of age, the count left the parish school to enter college which he also frequented for three months out of twelve. In summer time, the Count was travelling with the most famous shows, such as : Barnum & Bailey, Sells Bros., Forepaugh & Sells. In winter, he filled engagements with the greatest vaudeville circuits.

At the early age of three, his parents consented to let him travel with the greatest circus in the world. He was then accompanied by a member of his family and received a very large salary. Every year, his salary doubled and the midget had the privilege of selling his photo to his personal benefit, which brought him a larger sum than the salary itself.

Count Philippe Nicol gay and full of natural will was fond of travelling, highly esteemed by his employers and cheerished by the crowds which he entertained daily. He was admired everywhere on account of his small stature and also for his bright conversation, enlivened with wit and shrew with prompt and sharp rejoinders.

When he reached the age of fifteen, the count had enough experience to travel alone, and took on himself the management of his own affairs, in fact, he is remarkably qualified. Endowed with an alert mind and a prompt intellect, he masters very quickly the details of any question, and experience has proved that success has always favored him.

With such natural gifts it is no wonder that he thought himself fit for a business career and felt the ambition of making his fortune in a commercial enterprise ; so later, we find him at the head of a firm which he directed during fourteen years, at Manchester, N. H., the firm "Philippe Nicol" which enjoyed a world wide reputation under his management.

During this successful business period, Count Nicol, through the medium of Mr. Champagne, manager of our canadian champion of all strong men, Louis Cyr, made the acquaintance with Miss Rose Dufresne, of Lowell, Mass., herself of Lilliputian size, daughter of Carolus Dufresne, and grand daughter of P. Gagnon, of Yamachiche, P. Q. Mlle Dufresne was born in Lowell, June 17th 1887 ; she has three sisters and one brother, all of normal height.

Nous portons une attention spéciale aux poupées envoyées par malle ou express.

Special attention to dolls sent by Mail or Express

SALLE DES POUPEES
Le meilleur et le plus grand hôpital de poupées du Canada.

DOLLS' ROOM
Canada's best and largest Dolls' Hospital.

SALON
Longueur 7 pds. Largeur 7 pds. Hauteur 7½ pds.

PARLOR
Length 7 feet. Width 7 feet. Height 7½ feet.

With such aptitude, fitness for business and optimism , after a short courtship, he sued for the hand of Mlle Dufresne, from her tutor, Mr. P. Gagnon, who agreed with our Midget's desire without the slightest hesitation, knowing that the record of his past life was the best guarantee of his future behaviour.

The wedding ceremony was performed with great pomp on November 21st, 1906, at the church of St. Joseph,. Lowell, and the happy midgets were united in marriage by Reverend Father Amyot, O. M. I. It was a memorable day for the town's annals and never in men's memory had such a big crowd gathered as was seen on this occasion. Many business houses as well as numerous factories closed their doors while the ceremony lasted.

After a few weeks honey-moon trip, the happy spouses returned to Manchester, to live in a very fine house built especially according to the Count's specifications and plans, for himself and his beloved wife.

Nevertheless, after a few years work in his store, the Count was again seized with

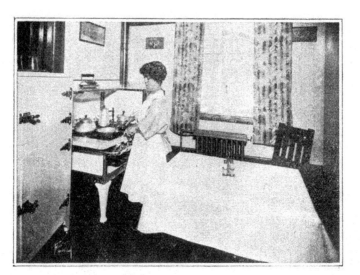

CUISINE

Longueur 10 pds.   Largeur 8 pds.   Hauteur 7½ pds.

KITCHEN

Length 10 feet.   Width 8 feet.   Height 7½ feet.

SALLE DE POOL ET DE BILLARD

Longueur 10 pds.   Largeur 10 pds.   Hauteur 7½ pds.

POOL AND BILLIARD ROOM

Length 10 feet.   Width 10 feet.   Height 7½ feet.

his passion for travelling, he, the man who had already circled the globe seven times. So he started again with his wife and travelled successfully in the Southern States and even in Europe with the biggest circusses.

In 1913, the Count decided to settle in Montreal. He started again in business very modestly at first, but his progress was so rapid that he now owns a very prosperous establishment. The attraction of his "Midgets' Palace", envied by the largest cities of the world, is for a good deal the secret of his success.

The Count had been in Montreal only thirteen years when he decided to build his actual palace which stands on Rachel Street East only a few steps from the west end corner of Lafontaine Park.

A visit to the present palace leaves a deep and pleasant impression on the visitor's mind ; but it is not exactly what the Count has dreamed of ; his greatest wish

would have been to erect right in the cen-
tre of Lafontaine Park, in the midst of
beautiful green lawns, fresh water pools,
shady driveways, colorful flowers, one of
the most costly buildings in the Canadian
metropolis, for the Count has always been
a lover of beautiful surroundings and acti-
vity.

In spite of his reiterated negotiations
with the Executive Committee of the City
it has been impossible to come to an agreement.

However, in their new palace, happiness
was not complete, somebody was missing
to this couple, to whom fortune had otherwise been constantly smiling : that was an
heir. The heir, object of their most ardent
wishes for twenty years, was born to them
on the 19th of September 1926. Bearing
the names of his father, C. P. Nicol, Junior,
weighed but three pounds and a half at
birth. He is perfectly constituted, very
lively and normal in every respect but size,
just as his parents themselves.

If to-day, Count Nicol is somewhat lame, this is due to rhumatism contracted in his prime youth, during the period of his no-mad life, with the circuses, when he had often to suffer from the inclemencies of the weather.

The five physicians who have assisted Countess Nicol at the birth of her baby by cesarian operation, at the Mercy Hospital, corner Dorchester and St. Hubert Streets, are of the opinion that he will be of still smaller size than his father, and that he will never be over thirty-five inches high.

Count and Countess Nicol are the only dwarves in the world who have given birth to a viable child. This child will be proud to say that he has the smallest parents in the world.

The Count is very firm in his desire to save his son from the hardships encountered by himself. He wishes to make of him, a serious, honest and charitable citizen, which is not common now adays.

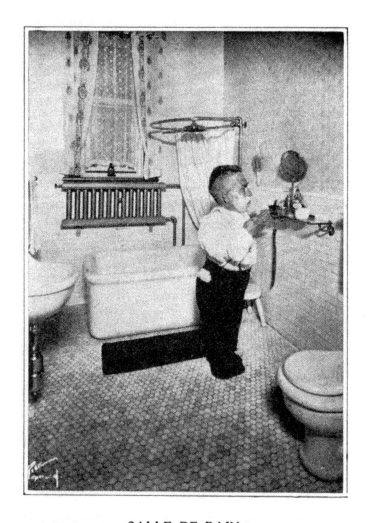

SALLE DE BAIN

Longueur 7 pds. Largeur 5 pds. Hauteur $7\frac{1}{2}$ pds.

BATH ROOM

Length 7 feet. Width 5 feet. Height $7\frac{1}{2}$ feet.

His education training will be that of a real business man ; he will endeavour rather to make of him a man like his father, always inclined to teach others the way of progress.

The Count's ideal for his son is nothing less than to see him attain the high intellectual qualities of our great and regretted Canadian statesman : Sir Wilfrid Laurier, the man with the unrivalled genius. He firmly expects for the next twenty years to put forth all his efforts to attain this object and nothing will be spared in time, efforts and money to make Nicol Jr. a real he man.

In the meantime, the Count is now perfectly happy with his wife and baby, and the days pass by very blessfully in a sweet matrimonial contentment.

Count Nicol is the richest dwarf in the world, charitable and obliging. He knows that richness are not only the consequence of skilful work, but also a gift from Him who has first bestowed upon us our natural qualities.

| THE PRINCE ROOM | LA CHAMBRE DU PRINCE |

| THE COUNT PHILIP NICOL Jr.
 The Rare Child in a room of prince at three years. He was born after 20 years of marriage. He is the only child born to midget parents. | LE COMTE PHILIPPE NICOL Jr
 L'Enfant Rare dans une chambre de prince à 3 ans. Il est né après 20 ans de ménage. Il est le seul enfant né de parents nains. |

| "19 SEPTEMBRE 1926"
 Le Comte et la Comtesse NICOL <br> avec leur trésor de Garçon et <br> les sept médecins, à la sortie de l'hôpital | "SEPTEMBER 26th 1926"
 Count and Countess NICOL <br> and there pretty boy <br> with the seven physicians, out of the hospital |

| Le Comte et la Comtesse Nicol à la sortie de l'hôpital un mois après la naissance de leur trésor de garçon le 19 octobre 1926, coin des rues Dorchester et Saint-Hubert. | Count and Countess Nicol out of the hospital one month after the birth of their pretty boy, October 19, 1926, corner Dorchester and Saint Hubert Sts. |

Salle d'Attente — 10 x 15 — Hauteur 10 pds. Intérieur de la Salle d'Attente où l'on peut se procurer un magnifique souvenir avec leur portrait.

Waiting Room — 15 x 10 — Height 10 feet. Interior of the Waiting Room where you can get a beautiful souvenir with their picture.

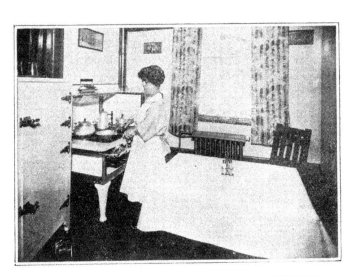

CUISINE

Longueur 10 pds. Largeur 8 pds. Hauteur 7½ pds.

KITCHEN

Length 10 feet. Width 8 feet. Height 7½ feet.

La COMTESSE NICOL, à l'âge de douze ans, pesant
seulement 25 lbs. et mesurant 26 pcs. de hauteur.
COUNTESS NICOL at twelve years of age, weighing
only 25 lbs, and 26 inches tall.

Le Comte Nicol, à 12 ans
Hauteur 25 pouces, Poids 25 lbs

Le COMTE NICOL, à l'âge de douze ans, pesant seulement 25 lbs, et mesurant 25 pcs de hauteur.
COUNT NICOL at twelve years of age, weighing only 25 lbs, and 25 **inches tall.**

VI.
CHARLES EISENMANN
PHOTOGRAPHS

C harles Eisenmann was the Richard Avedon of the Bowery, the downtown street that was lined with dime museums during New York's Gilded Age in the 1880s.

Eisenmann's work documenting the "freaks" of the era provides the foundation for much of what is known about these performers and their work. The traveling "midget shows" of the first half of the twentieth century were among the theatrical heritage Eisenmann preserved. His photographs helped to establish popular mythology about Little People and other "freaks."

His large-format camera captured the personalities of his subjects, and the sepia-toned paper available at the time gave the images sold in his studio a timeless quality even when they were new. Eisenmann's photographs were available as *cartes de visite* (or CdVs), photographs printed on small cards for the commercial market. Later, they would be replaced by *cabinet cards*. The mass production of these photos, and their continued ubiquity in public and private collections, has ensured the survival of the historic contributions made by Eisenmann and his subjects.

The following pages reproduce a selection of Charles Eisenmann's photographs of Little People, all dating to the late nineteenth century. We are grateful to the Ronald G. Becker Collection of Charles Eisenmann Photographs, Special Collections Research Center, Syracuse University Library, for permission to include these examples of Eisenmann's work.

Jim R. Moore

DUDLY FOSTER.
Age 5 years,   Weight 5 pounds.

DUDLY FOSTER
(CARTE DE VISITE)

MAJOR ATOM
(CABINET CARD)

Col. Steere & Wife,

229 BOWERY, N. Y.

COL. STEERE AND WIFE
(CABINET CARD)

LUCIA ZARATE WITH UNIDENTIFIED MAN
(CABINET CARD)

PRINCESS LUCY
(CABINET CARD)

ROSIE WOLFF
(CABINET CARD)

Eisenmann, Photo- 229 Bowery, N.Y

MAGGIE MINETT
(CARTE DE VISITE)

ADAMS SISTERS
(CARTE DE VISITE)

WILDMEN OF BORNEO
(CARTE DE VISITE)

THE GERMAN MIDGETS
(CARTE DE VISITE)

GENERAL RICKENBACK AND PRINCESS LUCY
(CABINET CARD)

MAJOR LITTLEFINGER AND WIFE
(CABINET CARD)

MAJOR RAY
(CABINET CARD)

MURAYS MIDGETS AND MOTHER
(CABINET CARD)

The Murays Midgets,
Tripplet Brothers,   Age 19 years.

THE MURAYS MIDGETS
(CARTE DE VISITE)

BIBLIOGRAPHY

Bogdan, Robert
Freak Show
University of Chicago Press, 1988

Fiedler, Leslie
*Freaks: Myths and Images of the Secret
    Self*
Simon & Shuster, 1978

Hartzman, Mark
American Sideshow
Tarcher/Penguin, 2005

Hunter, Jack
Freak Babylon
Creation Publishing, 2014

Mannix, Daniel P.
Freaks: We Who Are Not as Others
Pocket Books, 1971; Re/Search
    Publishing, 1990

Mitchell, Michael
*Monsters of the Gilded Age: The
    Photography of Charles Eisenmann*
Gage Publishing Limited, 1979

Nichell, Joe
Secrets of the Sideshow
University of Kentucky, 2005

Raabe, Meinhardt
Memories of a Munchkin
Back Stage Books, 2005

Roth, Hy and Cromie, Robert
The Little People
Beaverbooks, 1980

Skinner, Tina and Martin, Mary L.
*Midget Exhibit: Images from the Heyday
    of Dwarf Display*
Schiffer Publishing, 2004

Sloan, Mark and Tegge, Timothy Noel
*Wild, Weird and Wonderful: The
    American Circus as seen by F. W.
    Glasier*
Quantuck Lane Press, 2003

Taylor, James and Kotcher, Kathleen
Shocked & Amazed
Dolphin-Moon Press, 2018

ABOUT THE AUTHORS

TRAV S.D.

Writer and performer Trav S.D. is the author of *No Applause, Just Throw Money: The Book That Made Vaudeville Famous* (Faber & Faber, 2005), and *Chain of Fools: Silent Comedy and Its Legacies from Nickelodeons to Youtube* (Bear Manor Media, 2013). Since 2008 he has created the popular show biz blog Travalanche (travsd.wordpress.com), which has profiled thousands of historic vaudeville, burlesque and sideshow performers, actors, comedians, etc. He launched his American Vaudeville Theatre in 1995, and is proud to have produced and directed the NYC Fringe premiere of Noah Diamond's adaptation of the Marx Brothers' first Broadway show *I'll Say She Is* in 2014.

JAMES TAYLOR

In 1995, the first year of its publication, James Taylor's *Shocked and Amazed! On & Off the Midway* became the first journal to chronicle the history of novelty and variety exhibition, "the show business." Focusing on the sideshows and 19th Century dime museum entertainment, the journal also covers vaudeville and burlesque, wax museums and world's fairs, carnivals, circus spectacles, roadside attractions and everything in between. The journal features interviews with the business' "golden age" and modern performers and includes original works by the likes of Teller and Frank DeFord and unique reprinted material available previously to only a select few. *Shocked and Amazed!* has been recognized as the leading journal on the business in such venues as The Learning Channel, the History Channel, E! Entertainment Television, Channel 4 in London, the National Geographic Channel and *The Jerry Springer Show*. Taylor is a regular speaker at conferences and conventions focusing on the business as well as lecturing for a wide variety of groups at universities, private clubs and others interested in "weirdness as entertainment."

CPSIA information can be obtained
at www.ICGtesting.com
Printed in the USA
BVHW081244010421
603931BV00008B/499